SPOKESMAN FOR FREEDOM

THE LIFE OF ARCHIBALD GRIMKÉ

SPOKESMAN FOR FREEDOM

THE LIFE OF ARCHIBALD GRIMKÉ

Janet Stevenson

ILLUSTRATIONS BY JOHN WAGNER

CROWELL-COLLIER PRESS

Collier-Macmillan Limited / London

Library of Congress Catalog Card Number: 73-82561

The Macmillan Company
Collier-Macmillan Canada Ltd., Toronto, Ontario

Printed in the United States of America

First Printing

1715192

CONTENTS

SPOKESMAN FOR FREEDOM

THE LIFE OF ARCHIBALD GRIMKÉ

1

FROM FREEDOM TO SLAVERY

The three Grimké boys were the best fighters on Coming Street.

Archy was twelve and small for his age, but he could kick harder than anyone in the neighborhood. Frank, who was a year younger and nearly as big, could bite like a wildcat. John was only eight, going on nine, but he could butt harder than an angry billy goat. When all three of the brothers fought together, there was no gang of white boys in Charleston who could give them a beating.

In the beginning their mother had forbidden them

to fight. Mauma's word was law to her sons. She was strict but they knew she loved them, for she worked from dawn until long after dark, day after day, to keep hunger and cold and sickness from the little wooden house that was their home.

The two older boys helped her as much as they could. Mauma did washing and ironing for rich people who lived in the fine houses at the other end of Coming Street and on the Battery overlooking Charleston's harbor. She needed plenty of water, and the public pump was a quarter of a mile away. So twice a day Archy and Frank carried the pails to be filled. They also delivered clean clothes and brought back dirty ones in their little wooden wagon. Sometimes the white ladies gave Archy the money to bring home to Mauma.

There were gangs of white boys on Coming Street who sometimes lay in wait for Archy and Frank and jumped on them. If the boys were carrying water, they had no hands left to defend themselves, for each carried one pail in his outside hand, and they shared the third pail between them. It didn't matter so much when all they lost was water. The bad times were when the white boys overturned the little wagon and dumped out the clean clothes, or stole the money Archy was bringing home.

Mauma didn't like having to wash the clothes all

over again, and she didn't like seeing the scratches and bruises on her boys' faces and arms and legs. Finally, she told them that they could fight to defend themselves if they were attacked, but they were never to strike the first blow, no matter what might be said to make them angry.

After that they had very little trouble. It took only a few battles, using the kicking-biting-butting system, to spread word that the Grimké boys had better be left alone.

Archy and Frank could both read and write. It was something to be proud of and to keep secret.

There was a law in South Carolina at that time that made it a crime to teach such things to a Negro child. The Grimké boys had gone to school for a while, studying with an old Negro woman who was brave enough to risk punishment for teaching them their letters and numerals. Later, for a few months, they went to a school that had a white schoolteacher who was hired by some free Negro fathers to teach their sons. Then someone reported the school to the police and it was closed. But by that time the boys had learned enough to go ahead on their own.

The best thing about their lives was that they were free.

Most of the black children they saw on the streets of Charleston were not. They were slaves belonging to white masters and mistresses, rich people like the ones Mauma worked for. Sometimes these boys were better dressed and better fed than Archy and Frank, but the Grimké boys would not have changed places with them for anything in the world.

Slaves could be bought and sold like pigs and chickens and cows!

Archy had found that out back on Cane-Acres, the rice plantation in the back country where he and Frank were born. They lived in Mauma's little house across the yard from the big house with white pillars where Massa lived. Massa was a white man who owned Cane-Acres and everything on it. All the black people who worked there had to do what he said, or what another white man called the overseer said. All but Mauma! If she and the overseer disagreed about something, they would go to Massa about it, and sometimes he would decide that Mauma was right and tell the overseer to do as she said.

There was another thing about Mauma that was different. She raised pigs and chickens. None of the other black people did that. Sometimes a few of the animals would disappear, and Archy would ask about them. Mauma would say they had been taken into Charleston and sold, and she would show him the money she got for them.

Then one day Massa died and everything was to be sold!

Archy had liked Massa—a tall, thin man with gray-blue eyes, the color of a hawk's, and bushy eyebrows like tufts of tree moss. They had played a game together, Massa and he. Archy would come to the bottom of the steps that led up to the porch of the big house and pretend to be a horse, making a funny whinnying noise. Massa would come out and stand at the top of the steps and throw down whatever he had in his hand.

If it was a lump of sugar, Archy would gobble it up and make the horse sound again. But if it was a top Massa had whittled, or a marble, or a whistle, Massa would tell Horse to go find Archy and give the present to him. Archy would laugh and gallop off, still pretending to be Horse.

One day when Archy went to play the game, someone told him Massa was sick. Mauma stayed up at the big house all day and most of the night, nursing him. Someone else stayed with Archy and Frank, and whoever it was told them what would happen if Massa should die.

Everything would be sold! The houses and barns and the rice crop, and the horses and cows and pigs and chickens. And the people, too! All the black men and women and children who lived and worked on Cane-Acres!

Archy could hardly believe it, but the next day everyone on the plantation was quiet and frightened looking. Massa was dead, they said in whispers. The day after that white men came from Charleston and began taking things away.

Archy and Frank ran to Mauma, crying and begging her not to let the white men take them. Mauma hushed them and said they were not to worry. They were going to the city, but not because they were to be sold.

"We are free," Mauma told Archy. "Massa made us free in his will."

She told him that she was going to use the money that came from selling her pigs and chickens to buy boards to build a house for them. Uncle Owen Weston was giving her a place on the back of his lot on Coming Street. The new house would be better than the one they were leaving on Cane-Acres. The boys would go to school and learn a trade, and they would never be bought and sold like other black children they knew. Neither would they ever have to serve white people as slaves did.

Mauma promised them this and they trusted her.

When they first moved in to Charleston, the boys and Mauma lived with a white family, who were also named Grimké, at the upper end of Coming Street. Archy remembered almost nothing about those days except that his little brother, John, was born while they lived there.

When their own house was ready, Mauma and

her boys moved into it, and Archy and Frank only saw the white Grimkés when they went to deliver laundry. If they wondered why their own name was Grimké instead of Weston, like Mauma's kinfolk, someone probably told them it was because Mauma had once been a slave belonging to Henry Grimké. He was the father of young Mr. Montague Grimké and the brother of Miss Eliza—the two white Grimkés who lived in the Charleston house.

When slaves were freed, they often took the name of their ex-masters, especially if there was affection between them. But there was no affection between Mauma and the white Grimkés on Coming Street.

She did Mr. Montague's shirts and was paid for it, just as she was paid by other white families for whom she worked. When times were hard and there wasn't enough food, or enough wood to keep the little house warm, Mauma neither asked nor received help from the Grimkés. If her own kinfolk and neighbors couldn't help her, she and the boys went without.

That was why the boys didn't understand at first what Miss Eliza Grimké was talking about the day she invited them into the house. They had come with the laundry, as usual, but instead of paying them and giving them a basketful of soiled shirts to take home, Miss Eliza told them to come in and wash their hands and faces.

"I want you to look nice when you meet your new mistress," she said.

The boys thought they must have misheard her, but they washed their hands and faces and rubbed them dry on the towel Miss Eliza had put out for them. They were considering whether they should also wash their bare, dusty feet when Miss Eliza came back.

"When you meet her, you are to bow," she said. "Make a little bob with your heads, scrape your right foot back, and say 'How de do, mistress. How glad we are to see you!' "

The boys followed Miss Eliza up to the parlor on the second floor where Mr. Montague was sitting with a very pretty young lady in a fluffy lavender dress. Miss Eliza gave them a little shove forward. They bobbed their heads and scraped their feet, but they would not say those silly meaningless words about being glad to see a mistress.

As soon as they could, they ran home to tell Mauma what had happened and to ask her what it meant.

Mauma looked as if she had a terrible pain, like a bad toothache. She asked them to tell her twice over what Miss Eliza had said, what Mr. Montague had done or said, and what the young lady had looked like.

"That must be Miss Julia, Montague's new wife,"

Mauma said. But that was all. She didn't explain anything, and after a while the boys forgot to be curious.

A week later, Mauma told Archy that he was to go and serve in Mr. Montague's house.

The boy was too surprised to be angry at first. He did as he was told, listened to Miss Eliza explaining his duties to him—how he was to lay the table for family meals, chop wood and start fires in the grates in every room, and run errands for Miss Julia. She showed him how the knives and forks and spoons were to be placed, and the napkins and silver and plates. Archy tried to do exactly as she did. He wanted to please her because he had some idea that this was work for which he would earn money to help Mauma.

But late in the afternoon, Miss Julia called him upstairs to show him the new suit of clothes he was to wear while he was on duty in the Grimké house.

It was made of fine gray wool, and it had two rows of brass buttons down the front. Archy knew what sort of suit it was. Livery, it was called. And it meant that whoever wore it was a house servant—a slave!

He ran all the way home that evening and burst in on Mauma who was ironing in the kitchen.

"Howcomeso you told us we never going to have to serve?" he asked. "You said we free!"

Mauma nodded. She still had that look of pain, and she used as few words as she could to tell him what had happened.

Massa—Henry Grimké—was his father! His father and Frank's and John's!

Mauma had once been the housekeeper of the white Grimké family when they lived in a fine house in Charleston. When Mrs. Grimké fell sick, it was Mauma who nursed her, and Mrs. Grimké had begged Mauma to look after the three children she was leaving when she died. Mauma had carried out that trust. She had been a real mother to all of them, including Montague, who was the oldest.

When the youngest was old enough to be sent away to boarding school, Massa had taken Mauma away from Charleston, out to Cane-Acres. There she had borne him two sons before his death and another a few weeks after it.

Under the laws of South Carolina, Massa could not make her and her sons legally free. But when he lay dying, he told Mauma that he was leaving her better than free.

"I have written it in my will that you and the boys are to be under Montague's care. He's to see that you never want for anything. To treat you like one of his own family."

Massa trusted his oldest son to carry out that

promise, but Montague had betrayed the trust. He had not treated Mauma as a slave at first. He had let her sell her barnyard animals and keep the money. No slave could do that. But except for giving them shelter when they first came to Charleston, the white Grimkés had done nothing at all for the Negro family that went by the same name.

Mauma was bitter, but she was powerless to protect Archy. The law said he—and both of his brothers, as well as Mauma herself—belonged to Montague. There was nothing Mauma or the boys could do, except to run away.

Archy was still too little for that, Mauma said.

2

THE WAR WITHIN THE WAR

The new life that began for Archy was not as hard in some ways as the old one had been, but he hated it.

There was plenty to eat, the work was not hard, and he could go home every night to Mauma and his brothers in the little house at the other end of Coming Street. But Archy couldn't get used to being a slave.

That shameful suit with brass buttons reminded him every time he wore it. When his old playmates saw him, running an errand for Miss Julia, they mocked him as he had once mocked other slave boys. He wanted to run and hide. Or run away to freedom. If only he knew where it was!

At first he hoped that if he didn't learn to be a good servant, the Grimkés might change their minds and let him go. So he pretended to be stupid. He did as Miss Eliza told him while she was watching, but as soon as he was left alone to do anything, he mixed it all up.

Sometimes he was punished with a blow from a slipper—not hard enough to hurt him, but enough to hurt his pride. Sometimes the Grimkés sent him home and told Mauma to punish him. She never whipped him, but she looked worried—almost sick. That punished Archy worse than a whipping, but still he couldn't make up his mind to be a good, obedient slave.

Sometimes he felt that he was fighting a war, a small private war of his own inside the big war that was going on in the world outside.

That war was between the southern states, like South Carolina and her neighbors, and the states in the north. Archy and Frank had actually seen the big war begin.

One night there was a great excitement in Charleston. Everybody was running down to the Battery to look out over the harbor toward Fort Moultrie. All

of a sudden there was a long red streak across the sky, like fireworks. Then a noise like thunder. Then more fireworks.

The cannons from Fort Moultrie were shooting at the little island of Fort Sumter, where the Yankees were. Yankees were northerners and most people in Charleston seemed to hate them. Even so Archy didn't understand why there should be a war against them, so he asked his Uncle Owen.

The south was breaking away to start a new country, Uncle Owen said, and the north was fighting to stop it from doing so. The trouble was something to do with slavery. If the north won, all the slaves would be free. If the south won, free colored people like Uncle Owen and Big Aunty would be made slaves.

Next morning all the white people in Charleston were as proud and happy as if it were Christmas and the Fourth of July at the same time. Mauma and the Westons and all the rest of Mauma's kinfolk and friends were quiet and worried-looking. There was a new flag instead of the old one with the stars and stripes. And always, from then on, talk of battles.

The white people who came to the Grimkés' house talked as if the south was winning. Montague and his friends seemed to think the war would be over soon, and times would be better for everyone. Negroes Archy knew felt just the opposite, but they had to hide their feelings. Only when they were out of sight and hearing of white people did they talk freely.

When Archy heard that kind of talk, it was almost all about escaping from slavery. If the north won, people said, there would be no need to run away. Everyone would be free. But that might not happen for a long time. Some were too impatient to wait. They took the first chance they got to slip away, cross the marshes, and make their way to a camp of Union troops.

There was such a camp out on the sand islands near the mouth of Charleston Harbor. Every week there was a rumor that another group of slaves had found their way to freedom by that short-cut. But Mauma said Archy was still too young for such a journey.

He could only wait and hope and keep fighting his own small, private war.

Then one day the Grimkés sent for Frank.

Now there were two soldiers in the private war. In some ways it was better. Archy had missed his brother and was glad to be with him more of the day, but it was not like being together in the old free life. There was no time for games.

Also, Frank got into much worse trouble with the

Grimkés right from the start, and that made more and worse trouble for Mauma.

Frank was always running away. Every time he was set to some chore he hated, like cleaning Montague's muddy boots, for instance, he would wait until Miss Eliza's back was turned and then be off. He always ran to Mauma and Mauma had to bring him back.

There was nothing else she could do. If a slave ran away from his master in Charleston, a constable was sent to arrest him and take him to the workhouse—a terrible stone prison full of dark cells where slaves were chained up or beaten to teach them to be obedient and to work hard. Mauma didn't want that to happen to one of her sons. But Frank was too young to understand, and he couldn't forgive her for taking him back to Montague's house.

Mauma had that toothache look most of the time now, and she and Frank hardly spoke.

Something must have gone wrong with the plans for a quick southern victory for at about this time there was news of the Union winning battles at two places that sounded alike to Archy—Gettysburg and Vicksburg.

White people were beginning to suffer in ways they couldn't hide. Soldiers were coming home wounded or crippled. Many families wore black because someone they loved had been killed at the front. Even in the fine houses of Charleston there was not always enough to eat.

Negroes were even more careful than before not to show their true feelings in front of white people, but their hopes were rising. Archy's hopes were rising, too. He dreamed of a great army of Yankees sailing into Charleston harbor and a great shout of jubilee going up from a crowd of black people waiting to greet them. At other times he dreamed of getting a little boat and crossing the harbor some night, all by himself, or with Frank, and being greeted and freed by blue-coated soldiers.

His real life was getting harder all this time. Tempers in the Grimké household were getting shorter. It took only a small mistake to bring on punishment. And the punishments were getting crueler.

Frank got the worst of it as long as he was there. But one day the Grimkés decided they had had enough of him. Since neither they nor Mauma could teach him obedience, they hired him out to a man who was known for breaking the spirits of unruly slaves by hard work, beating, and starvation.

There was no coming home at night from this master. Frank disappeared and there was no word of him for weeks.

With Frank gone, it seemed as if the Grimkés had more time to find fault with Archy. Nothing he did was right. One morning when he couldn't get a fire started in the dining-room grate, and the family had to come down to breakfast in a cold room, Montague lost his temper, pulled off his house slipper, and began to beat Archy as hard as he could.

Archy began to scream.

"Make him stop that," Miss Julia told Mr. Montague. "Everyone in the neighborhood can hear him. It's a disgrace."

But Archy wouldn't stop screaming. The harder Montague beat him to make him stop, the louder he screamed, until they were both worn out.

Later that day a constable came and took Archy away to the workhouse. Montague was waiting for him there and gave directions to the jailer to have Archy whipped until he learned "not to make a fuss over nothing."

The boy was told to strip to the waist. His feet were locked into stocks on the stone floor. His arms were fastened to a pulley that drew them up over his head. A rough woolen cap was pulled down over his face so that he could hardly breathe, much less cry out. Then he was beaten with a leather strap until he could feel the blood running down his back.

"That's enough," Montague said at last.

The beating stopped. The cap was pulled off and the chains were loosened. Archy was told to get dressed and go home.

While Montague was counting out the money to pay for this punishment, Archy got his breath.

"Brother!" he said as loud as he could.

Montague and the jailer turned to look at him.

"That's right," Archy said. "It's his own brother he had this done to!"

Montague looked as if he wanted to beat Archy all over again, but he said nothing and went away.

Archy went home.

Mauma washed his wounds, put healing poultices on them, and put him to bed. But before he slept, Archy told her that he would never go back to the Grimkés after this. He would have to run away whether he was too little or not.

"First thing is to get well," Mauma said. "You can't do much running with a back like that."

Archy knew that she understood. She would not try to make him return to slavery. She would do all she could to help him escape when the time came.

3

THE DAY OF JUBILEE

Before Archy's back was entirely healed, Mauma had found a place for him to hide. It was way out on Line Street, in the home of a free Negro family named Cole.

The Coles were willing to keep him for a while, although they risked losing their own freedom by doing so. But Mauma told them it would not be for long. As soon as she heard of a group of runaways heading for the swamps, she would ask them to take Archy.

Meanwhile, the problem was how to get him safely to the Coles.

The Grimkés were already sending messages to ask when Archy was coming back to work. Mauma made excuses about his back being slow to heal, but one day Montague might come by to see for himself how his little slave boy was doing. Mauma wanted Archy gone by that time.

They talked over many plans for escape with his uncles and friends. One of them offered to hide Archy in a wagonload of cotton waste, drive him out to Line Street, and unload him after dark. In the end, however, the safest thing seemed to be the simplest. Archy and Mauma would walk the whole way, but Archy would be disguised so that no one would recognize him.

Much to Archy's embarrassment, Mauma borrowed clothes from neighbors who had daughters. He made his escape from the little house dressed as a girl!

Mauma chose a night when the moon came up very late, so she and Archy could make the trip in darkness but in the early hours of the night—before the constables were likely to stop people on the street and ask their business.

They were lucky. No one bothered them all the way out to the Coles!

There Mauma introduced him to his new friends, kissed him goodbye, and made him promise to do just what Uncle and Aunt Cole said, and to make himself helpful in every way he could.

The rules of this life of hiding were very strict, but Archy understood the reason and that made it easier to keep them. He was never to go outdoors in daylight, so that no one—not even friendly black neighbors—would know he was in the house. He could go out on moonless nights, but only into the backyard. If anyone came to visit—except, of course, Mauma—he was to hide in a closet until they left.

The window blinds were closed at night, but to close them by day might make people suspicious. So they were left open, and that meant Archy had to stay away from the windows. Whenever he passed one, he was to stoop so low that he couldn't be seen by anyone passing along the sidewalk.

The worst thing about this arrangement was that Archy had nothing to keep him busy. Time passed as slowly as a prison sentence until the Coles discovered that Archy knew how to read.

Then Uncle Cole began to bring home books and newspapers and asked Archy to read them aloud. The family would gather after supper every evening to listen, mostly to news about how the war was going.

Almost all the news was bad, but Uncle Cole said it was not all true. Also, not all the true news was told in the Charleston papers. A year ago, for instance, President Lincoln had proclaimed that all slaves in the states that were at war against the Union were free. But there had not been one word about the Emancipation Proclamation in any paper Uncle Cole had seen.

Uncle Cole got this news and lots more from other free colored people who kept their ears open and passed on what they heard. Archy learned in this way that things were not as simple as Uncle Owen had believed them to be back at the beginning of the war.

For one thing, not everyone in the north, or even in the Union Army, was the Negro's friend. Escaped slaves had been turned back by some commanders, even turned over to the southern masters from whom they had run away. Also, the Emancipation Proclamation gave freedom only to slaves in states that had rebelled against the Union. In others—states like Missouri and Kentucky—that were fighting on the Union side, men still had the right to own, to buy, and to sell other men.

Still, it seemed that the best hope black men had in these terrible times was the hope that the north would win the war.

The Coles followed each bit of news Archy read

aloud to them and tried to figure out the truth behind it. When it was too discouraging, they reminded each other that when things went badly for the south, news might be kept back so that southerners wouldn't lose heart. Perhaps that was what was happening right now.

One night Uncle Cole brought home a piece of news that impressed Archy so much that years afterward he almost believed he had seen it happen.

There had been a battle out near the harbor's mouth. Union soldiers had tried to storm the Confederate fort and been thrown back after many had been killed. Of the few Union prisoners taken alive and brought back to Charleston, most were Negroes! Black soldiers in the uniform of the Army of the United States! It was a sight to make southern white men angry and fearful, and black men hopeful and proud.

Now Archy had a new dream—to escape to the Union camp and enlist as a soldier! It might be that his brother, Frank, had already done that. Mauma brought word that Frank had run away from the brutal master to whom the Grimkés had hired him out. Was he already wearing the uniform of the armies of freedom? It was possible.

Days dragged by and made weeks, which slowly mounted into months, and finally there were twelve of them. A whole year since Archy had come to the

Coles! He was still hoping that Mauma would find a way for him to escape, but she had had no luck. Another month passed, and another. Six of them, and it was a year and a half since he had been outside the little house by day. Seven, eight, nine, ten. . . Soon it would be two whole years!

Then everything seemed to happen at once.

The war moved in from the islands to Charleston itself. Everyone in the city had always said the Yankees could never reach its buildings even with their biggest guns. But now there was a new gun, a huge cannon that sent shells into those parts of the city where the richest white people lived. Houses were destroyed, and fires were started that destroyed more houses.

Not many shells fell near Mauma's house nor near the Coles, but once Mauma was nearly killed on the streets when she was coming to see Archy.

And there were terrible rumors running through the neighborhoods. People said that the Confederate cavalry regiments under Colonel Wheeler were going to burn all the cotton stored in the warehouses along the waterfront. This was to be done to keep the Yankees from capturing the cotton if they came into the city. That was bad enough, but now there was a worse rumor—that all the ammunition in all the arsenals in the city was to be blown up.

Panic sent people running in all directions, trying to get out of the way of the explosions. Some tried to get away by boat, but most tried to escape inland. The one narrow road leading out of Charleston was soon so clogged with wagons full of household goods that no one could get through, even on foot.

The leading men of the city met in the mayor's office to decide what to do. It seemed to them that it was more important to save Charleston and its people than to keep things from falling into the Yankees' hands. So the city fathers crowded into a small, open boat, flying a white flag of truce, and went out to talk to the commander of the Union gunboats just outside the harbor's mouth.

At their invitation, the Yankees came in to save the city they had besieged so long.

Everyone in the Coles' neighborhood went down to the Battery to watch the Union troops land. It would be just like Archy's dream—a great shout of jubilee from thousands of black throats! For when the old Stars and Stripes flew again over Charleston all slaves would be free.

Archy wanted to see that happen, but after two years he wasn't ready to go out-of-doors in daylight. He wasn't afraid exactly, but he had to get used to the idea a little at a time.

When he finally ventured out, everything was very

quiet. He began to walk slowly toward the center of the city, stopping now and then to figure out where he was.

So much had changed. There were whole blocks of rubble where fine homes had been. There was grass growing between the paving stones of the main streets. And there were soldiers everywhere. Their uniforms were so faded that it was hard to tell whether they were gray or blue, Confederate or Union. They were clearing the streets, putting out fires, unblocking the sewers, bringing the city back to life. But there was not a single face that Archy recognized, black or white.

Then he saw Frank.

He was riding with a Yankee officer, wearing a new blue uniform and a fine new cap trimmed with buttons and braid. He had a rifle and his horse was fat and shiny.

Archy stared and stared, trying to decide whether it was really his brother or part of a dream. He didn't say a word. But Frank turned as if he had heard his named called. He met Archy's eyes and smiled.

Then it was all real.

The brothers had found each other in freedom and the day of jubilee had begun.

4

WHAT IS FREEDOM?

Archy wanted to join the army that was bringing freedom into South Carolina. After being locked up for so long, he wanted to move around. And he wanted to do something on his own to win the freedom he had dreamed about for so long.

Frank was able to get a place not only for Archy but also for two of their cousins, young Owen Weston and Frank O'Hear. There was a real need for young men who knew the countryside and could ride with the Union troops, for Wheeler's cavalry was still hiding out in the woods and swamps, and it was not going to be easy to clear them out.

Each of the cousins served a different Yankee officer, but they were always close enough to meet and cook their evening meal together and compare notes on the day's excitement. It was a hard life and sometimes an ugly one. Archy didn't mind the hardships or the danger as much as he did the feeling of shame for some of the things the soldiers did.

He didn't blame them for taking what they needed to eat. But they destroyed more than they could use. In this way they were no better than Wheeler's cavalry, which had tried to destroy everything the enemy might get and use. And the people who would suffer were farm women and children. Archy knew from experience the hunger pangs these people would feel before there was a new harvest to replace what was being stolen or slaughtered or burned.

Little by little, war lost its glamour for the boys. Sleeping night after night in wet clothes with no shelter but a soggy blanket weakened their resistance. One by one they came down with "chills and fever" and had to be sent home.

Archy lasted the longest, but in the end he too came home for Mauma to nurse.

Charleston was quite a different city by this time. A Mr. Gilbert Pillsbury of Boston had been appointed mayor, and one of the first things he had done was to reopen the schools—to children of all colors!

"All children in the city of Charleston are to attend the public school nearest their dwelling place," so his proclamation read.

For Archy and Frank and John this meant the Morris Street School, a big, two-story building that overlooked the little wooden shack where they and their cousins had gone to school in secret before the war.

On the day Mauma took her three sons up the steps, through the big doors, and into the school to register them as pupils, Archy felt that he was beginning at last to be really free.

For he knew now that freedom meant more than just not being a slave. All through the months when he had been a prisoner at the Coles', he had read in order to escape—at least in dreams. And reading had taught him how much he was missing by not being free.

Sometimes Archy thought of the world as a house full of locked doors. He and all the other black children of the south were locked out, not locked in. Freedom, when it came, would mean opening those doors and going into all those rooms. He wasn't sure what he would find, but he knew he must study hard to find out.

None of the three Grimké brothers liked being

cooped up all day, sitting on hard benches, copying spelling lists, and adding up sums. But Archy and Frank were willing to put up with it. John was not. And so, one day before the end of the first term, it was the two older boys who were sent for by the school's principal, Mrs. Pillsbury.

She was the wife of the mayor, and she too came from Massachusetts. The first thing she said to Archy and Frank was that she had noticed their name on the teacher's report because it was a familiar one. They didn't understand all she was saying because of her queer, Yankee way of talking, but they did catch the names, Angelina and Sarah Grimké, which meant something to them.   1715192

Miss Angelina and Miss Sarah were sisters of Miss Eliza, who had gone north before the war. Miss Eliza used to talk about them sometimes, and everything she said was bad. Now Mrs. Pillsbury was saying that these ladies had not only freed their own slaves, but done what they could to have all slaves freed. "Abolitionists," she called them.

Archy had heard that word spoken by white people who spat it out as if it tasted bad. He learned now that it meant people who wanted to abolish slavery. So there were Grimkés who were not to be hated! It was a new idea to Archy, hard to get used to, but worth thinking about.

Before he could do much thinking, however, Mrs.

Pillsbury said something that drove everything else
out of his mind. She thought he and Frank deserved
a better education than they could get in Charleston!
How would they like to go north to school? Would
their mother consent to letting them go?

Mauma was almost as excited as Archy and Frank
by Mrs. Pillsbury's offer. She never praised her sons
to their faces, but after she had talked to Mrs. Pillsbury, she was so proud that she forgot to hide it.

The principal had spoken of the leaders that
would be needed as the Negro people took their
place as citizens in a democracy. Archy and Frank
had the makings of such leaders, she believed, and
that was why she was ready to do all she could to
see that they got the education they would need to
play their parts well.

With Mauma's consent, Mrs. Pillsbury was already writing letters to friends in Boston, asking
them to make arrangements. The boys were to live
with a white family while they went to school. They
would be expected to do some work in exchange for
their board and room, but not enough to interfere
with their studying. If they did well, they could go
on to college and train to be doctors, lawyers, min-
isters, teachers—whatever career they chose for
themselves!

It was too much to hold in their hearts. Mauma

knelt down and the boys did the same. Together they prayed, gave thanks, and asked God's help to be equal to the great chance they were being given.

It took only a week or so for the rumor to spread all over Charleston, and folks started dropping in to the little house to ask if it was true.

Not everyone who came believed that Mauma was doing right in letting the boys go so far from home. They were too young to be sent a thousand miles away to a place where they had no kinfolk or friends. Northern people weren't all such great friends of the black man as the Pillsburys seemed to be. What was wrong with the schools right here in Charleston? And how was Mauma going to get on without her two oldest sons?

The last was the question that worried Archy. Mauma never showed her feelings, but he knew how it must be hurting her to lose the two she had just got back after so long. But what Mauma wanted for her boys was always more important to her than what she wanted for herself. She listened politely to all the questions and warnings, but she never gave any sign of changing her mind and saying the boys couldn't go.

Before the end of summer, Mrs. Pillsbury had everything settled. Frank, who had decided he wanted to be a doctor, was to live with a Dr. John

Brown in Stoneham, Massachusetts, and study medicine with him. Archy was to live in Boston with a Mr. Sewell. It was too bad the boys couldn't be together, but the distance between Boston and Stoneham was not so great that they couldn't get to see each other every now and then.

The day of parting came in late September. Archy and Frank put on their new trousers and jackets—too heavy for the hot Carolina weather, but not quite heavy enough for what they might find in Massachusetts by the time they got there. Mauma packed a satchel with their extra shirts, and a bar of her own brown soap for them to wash with. She kissed them and blessed them and shoved them out the door almost roughly.

As they headed down Coming Street, they didn't look back or wave. They didn't even look at each other, just straight down at their feet that were hurrying toward the Battery. There they were to meet Mrs. Pillsbury and be put aboard a boat that would take them to Port Royal, where they were to wait for the boat that would take them all the way up to New York.

Archy was sixteen years old, too near a grown man to cry over leaving home. But he didn't want to take a chance on bringing tears to Frank's eyes . . . or to Mauma's . . .

5

NORTH TO DISAPPOINTMENT

At the army camp on the island of Port Royal, the boys were the guests of Major Martin Delaney, a very black man, darker even than Mauma, who was darker than any of her sons. Major Delaney spent a lot of time with Archy and Frank and told them a good deal of what they would find different in the great cities of New York and Boston. They listened to everything he said, but the most important thing they learned from him was the story of his own life.

Martin Delaney's childhood had been as hard as

the Grimké boys'. Yet he had educated himself, got into Harvard College, which was the best in the whole country, become a doctor, published a newspaper, written books, traveled all over the world, and risen to the highest rank so far held by a member of his race in the Army of the United States. He was living proof that their own dreams could come true.

When the gunboat that was to carry them north arrived at last, Major Delaney had orders to make the same voyage on other business. So Archy and Frank were not really on their on when they finally docked in New York.

Their new friend escorted them through the busy streets and saw them safely delivered to the offices of the Anti-Slavery Society. The pleasant gentlemen there seemed to be expecting them. One took the boys for a long walk to show them the sights of the great city. Another took them home for the night and introduced them to his family as if Archy and Frank were especially welcome and honored guests.

After a day of resting and more sightseeing, the boys were put on a train for Springfield, Massachusetts. This was their first railroad trip, and more interesting than the sea voyage because they could see the country through which they were passing. It was very different—greener and cleaner than the country around Charleston. Farms and people looked better cared for, better off.

In Springfield, they were met at the station by a Dr. and Mrs. Church, who took them home for the night, and asked if they would like to stay over an extra day and go to the theater.

Had the boys ever seen a stage play? They shook their heads. How would they like to hear the famous actor, Edwin Forrest, play in Shakespeare's tragedy of *King Lear*? Archy and Frank were not in such a hurry to get to the end of their journey that they could turn down a chance like this.

The words of the play were hard to understand, but the voice of the actor who played the old king got into Archy's head and heart. For many years afterward, even to think about that marvelous evening would start memories that made his throat tighten and his eyes sting.

There was no one to meet them at the station in Boston. Dr. Church had warned them that this might happen and had given them directions for finding the office of the Anti-Slavery Society where they were to get a ticket for Stoneham. Archy was to go with Frank and see him settled before going to his own place with Mr. Sewell, back in Boston.

For the first time the two brothers were really on their own. Boston was not as big or as bustling as

New York, but even so it was a little frightening to push their way through crowds of strangers and see not another dark face anywhere.

Archy was glad they didn't have to ask the way from anyone, and even gladder to see the words

ANTI-SLAVERY SOCIETY
FREEDMEN'S BUREAU

on the door of the office on the second floor of a building on Tremont Street, just up from the Commons.

The letter of introduction Archy was carrying was addressed to a Reverend Wentworth, who was in charge of that Bureau. But instead of a white gentleman in a clergyman's coat, it was a young Negro lady who sat behind the big desk.

Her name was Charlotte Forten, she told the boys. Reverend Wentworth had left her in charge because he had to leave the city for a few days. That was the first disappointment.

The second was more serious. Miss Forten was not expecting them. She had no instructions, no tickets to give them. It seemed that Reverend Wentworth had been in such a great hurry to get away that he had forgotten to leave word.

She was upset and uncertain about what to do.

Frank took a real dislike to her (something Archy was to tease him about years later) and refused her offer of a loan of the carfare. There was no reason, Frank said, why he and Archy couldn't walk.

"But Stoneham is twenty miles from here," Miss Forten said, as if that made it impossible.

It was true that the boys had walked that far more than once in their lives. But Archy didn't think this was the time to do it again. It was already late afternoon; it would soon be dark. Also it was cold and the sky looked like rain. Massachusetts was not South Carolina. Sleeping under a tree was not a pleasant prospect this far north in early November.

"Did you say your name is Grimké?" Miss Forten asked suddenly.

When Archy said yes, she got very excited and began talking about Miss Angelina and Miss Sarah, just the way Mrs. Pillsbury had talked about them. They lived here in Boston, and they had one of their sisters from Charleston visiting them. Miss Eliza Grimké! Perhaps Archy and Frank knew the lady?

Archy said nothing and Miss Forten went on. Why didn't the boys call on the famous sisters who would surely want to help them in any way they could. Mr. Sewell, the man Archy was going to stay with, was also a friend of the Grimkés'. If they were too shy to go alone, Mr. Sewell would be able to introduce them.

Archy had stopped listening.

As far as he was concerned this was the worst disappointment of all. He had not come all the way from Charleston to get mixed up with old Miss Eliza again. He wouldn't go near Miss Angelina or Miss Sarah, or even Mr. Sewell, so long as it meant taking a chance of running into his old enemy. He decided to ask Dr. Brown if there wasn't a place for him in Stoneham. That way he and Frank would be close enough to go to the same school for a while.

When Miss Forten saw that the boys were not willing to take her suggestion, she wrote out directions for the station where they would catch the train for Stoneham. Frank still didn't want to borrow the money from her, but she insisted that she would pay herself back when Reverend Wentworth returned.

They would have to hurry, she said, or they would miss the last train of the day. She wished them luck and asked them to write and tell her how they made out. But Frank muttered under his breath as they ran down the stairs that he would do no such thing.

Miss Charlotte Forten was too stuck up and schoolmarmy for his taste.

It was dark when the boys got off the train at Stoneham. But the first person they asked pointed to Dr. John Brown's house, and a few minutes later they were knocking at his door.

The doctor's office was right in his house. He was

seeing the last patient of the day when Archy and Frank arrived. They waited only a few minutes before he joined them, took the letter of introduction Frank had brought, and read it through carefully.

Dr. Brown was a pleasant, fatherly man whom Archy liked at first sight. But he took such a long time over the letter that both boys had begun to fidget before he was done. When he looked up at last, he was frowning in a way that made Archy's stomach knot with fear.

"I'm afraid there's been a misunderstanding here," he said. Mrs. Pillsbury had written him asking about a place for a young freedman. He had answered her, saying there was work enough around his place to keep a young man busy and a spare room where he could stay.

But there had been no further word from Mrs. Pillsbury. If she had written, her letter had been lost. In the meantime, the doctor's wife had hired a young girl to help her, and the girl was now using the spare room.

Worst of all, the doctor didn't see how Frank could study medicine here. Doctoring, he explained, was not a trade like blacksmithing or carpentry. A young man didn't learn it by apprenticing himself to an older man. At least not until he had gone through many years of college. There was no school in Stoneham where Frank could prepare to enter college, and no college at all.

Dr. Brown seemed honestly sorry for what had happened. He said he would write Mrs. Pillsbury and explain. While they were waiting to hear from her, Archy and Frank could stay on, if they didn't mind sleeping in the barn. They could earn their keep by looking after the doctor's horse and buggy, and making things ready in the garden for the winter that would be coming in a few weeks.

6

HALFWAY TO HOME

Archy and Frank made themselves as comfortable as they could in the loft above the horse's stall in the big drafty barn. They talked far into the night, trying to decide what to do.

They were a thousand miles from home, without a penny in their pockets or a friend to turn to. When Mrs. Pillsbury heard what had happened to her plans for them, Archy was sure she would try to make some other arrangements, but that might take weeks, even months. What should they do while they waited?

It was already almost too cold to stay in the loft. Besides, Frank didn't want to take any favors from the man who had disappointed him so badly. He hadn't come all this way, he said, just to water a horse and rake leaves and sleep in a pile of dusty hay. In the morning he was going to look for work somewhere else.

Archy decided he would, too. And he would not depend on Dr. Brown to let Mrs. Pillsbury know what had happened. He would write to Mauma and ask her to go to Mrs. Pillsbury with the bad news.

Frank was lucky enough to find work and a place to live with a family named Dykes, who lived just outside of Stoneham. Mr. Dykes farmed in the summer and made shoes in the winter. He was going to teach Frank to be a shoemaker. While he was learning, the boy was to have free room and meals. As soon as he was able to work on his own, he would get wages.

That part was fine. But the Dykes said just what Dr. Brown had about schooling. There were no schools in the neighborhood that would take a Negro student. It was worse in Massachusetts than it had been at home!

Archy had a harder time finding work, but at last

he did. One of Dr. Brown's patients who came up from Peacedale, Rhode Island, offered to take Archy back with her. He could work at her place for room and board, or he could find a job in one of the cotton mills in Peacedale. Archy hoped there might be a better chance of going to school there.

Peacedale was nearly fifty miles from Stoneham, and when the brothers said goodbye, each was really alone, and in what seemed like a foreign land.

As soon as Archy was settled, he began to ask about schools. There was one public grammar school in Peacedale, he was told. It was free. There was no rule that barred Negro pupils. But it was only for the primary grades.

Reading and writing and arithmetic were things Archy had already learned. Besides, the pupils were all so much younger than he was that Archy would have been embarrassed to sit at the same desks.

A young man his age ought to be going to a college, he was told. There was a fine one in Providence, a city almost the size of Boston, and only a few miles away. Were Negroes admitted? No one seemed to know. The best way to find out was to apply.

So Archy wrote to the admissions office of Brown University and asked for an application form. A week or so later, it came in the mail.

On one side of the paper were a lot of blanks to

fill in. He was to tell where he had lived before, what schools he had attended, what he had studied, and what grades he had received. On the other side of the page was a list of the subjects in which he would be examined before he could enter the freshman class.

Archy read it over once and gave up all hope.

Algebra up to quadratic equations! Reading and writing of Latin and Greek! A long list of books in those two dead languages! And more, much more.

What did it matter whether the college would admit a black student? Archy and Frank were too far behind ever to catch up. By the time they were ready to take examinations like that they would be old men! It had been a mistake ever to leave home.

If neither he nor Frank could hope to get into a college, they might as well forget their big dreams, and go home. There they could find work as good as what was offered here, and they would be near Mauma and John and their kinfolk and friends.

But how were they to get home? Neither he nor Frank was earning enough money to save the fare for a train or a ship. It was no use asking Mauma for it. And Mrs. Pillsbury had not yet answered their letters or Dr. Brown's.

November was past and the weeks of December were dragging by. Still no word from Charleston.

Even Mauma seemed to have forgotten them. Soon it would be Christmas. Archy had never been so discouraged before.

One day, while he was in this gloomy mood, he got a chance to ride in to Providence in one of the mill wagons. There he saw ships tied up along the river front, big oceangoing ships like those he had seen at the wharves along the Battery in Charleston.

Suddenly an idea came to him!

He could go to sea!

Up and down the waterfront he went, asking first one captain, then another, where his ship was bound, and whether he needed an extra deck hand. No one was going directly to Charleston, but some were heading for ports from which it might be possible to get another ship bound that way. And several of the captains said they could use extra hands!

All that held Archy back from signing on that very day was the thought of Frank. He couldn't go off and leave his brother without a word. Besides, Frank might want to come too.

Together they could make a real adventure out of such a voyage. Archy's spirits began to lift. He decided not to go back to Peacedale, but to head straight for Stoneham, find Frank, and offer him this way of escape from the prison without bars in which they were trapped.

Frank was not at the Dykes' when Archy arrived, cold and tired and almost famished. It had taken him two days and part of a third to make it on foot from Providence.

Mr. Dykes said that Frank had gone to Boston a day or so ago. There had been a letter for him, saying something about a school. The Dykes weren't sure of the details. Frank had gone to the Anti-Slavery Office to find out more.

When he opened the door of the Anti-Slavery Office, the first thing Archy saw was Frank, sitting at the desk with Miss Forten, and grinning at her as if they were the best of friends.

Reverend Wentworth was at his own desk this time. As soon as he saw Archy, he was on his feet, smiling and talking a blue streak about how fine it was that he had been able to get here so fast. Now Frank was talking, too. Archy could hardly make out what either of them was saying, but he knew that something like a miracle must have happened. Hope began to stir in him, like a bear waking from a winter's long sleep.

The miracle was that the brothers were to be sent to Lincoln University in Oxford, Pennsylvania.

The president of this college had written Mrs. Pillsbury and she had sent the letter on to Reverend Wentworth, who was reading it aloud to Archy now.

Because it was dedicated to the education of young men of all races, especially those who had been slaves, Lincoln University had a special preparatory class for students who were not ready to do college work.

"To enter this class we ask only that the applicant be able to read, write a fair hand, and know arithmetic through fractions," the letter said.

All the arrangements had been made. Reverend Wentworth had only been waiting for an answer to the letter he had sent Archy in Peacedale. Since Archy was here now, there was no reason to delay. The boys could catch a train this very afternoon.

When at last they were in their seats and had caught their breath, Archy asked Frank how far they were going. Where was Oxford, Pennsylvania?

Frank laughed and shook his head.

He didn't know for sure, but Mrs. Pillsbury had said in her letter that it was "almost halfway to home."

7

AUNT ANGELINA

Lincoln University didn't look like the boys' idea of a college, when they first saw it on a raw winter day. The campus was a newly cleared space on a low hill. Rows of spruce trees that would one day be tall and dignified were only bush-size now and pitifully scraggly.

There were two buildings besides the president's house. In one of them classes were held. In the other students ate and slept and studied.

President Randall, a white minister, talked to the

brothers and asked them all sorts of questions. They had to read aloud for him and show him how well they could write and do arithmetic. Finally, he gave his verdict.

They could have a year to show what they could do.

He was not sure it would be enough time for them to make up all the years they had lost, but it was all he could give them. There were too many other students who wanted the places Archy and Frank would be taking. Unless they could pass the entrance examinations at the end of the year, they would have to go back to Charleston and try the regular schools there.

It was up to them.

Archy and Frank worked harder than they had imagined anyone could.

They got up early in the morning and did their chores before breakfast, went to classes all day, and sat up late over their lessons every night. Sometimes they got discouraged, but they went on working anyway. They knew how foolish it would be to waste the chance they were getting.

At first they didn't seem to be learning very much or very fast. Sometimes Archy felt as if his head were a block of wood into which nothing more could be stuffed. But little by little his mind seemed to make room and take in new things, arrange and rearrange ideas, until they made patterns that made sense.

Studying got easier. Reading began to be exciting. The mysterious world of numbers and letters called "algebra" got to be a familiar place.

When examination time came, they were ready. They passed all their subjects—some with high grades, others not so high. But they passed!

President Randall called them in again and told them they had earned the right to stay on at Lincoln as freshman. If they went on working as hard and as well, they would graduate with honors, he believed.

Then he asked whether they had thought about their futures. What did they want to be when they finished college? For what sort of work did they want to prepare?

By this time Frank had decided he was no longer interested in becoming a doctor. He wanted to be a minister. Archy couldn't make up his mind whether he wanted to be a writer and to publish a newspaper like Major Delaney's, or whether he wanted to go into politics. He still remembered what Mrs. Pillsbury had said about representing his people in the government.

President Randall was pleased with both boys' answers. Archy would have to go to law school after he graduated from Lincoln, he said, and Frank, to a theological seminary. But there were things they could begin to study right away that would help them in their future careers. One of these was public speaking—oratory, as it was called then.

There was no regular course in this subject at Lincoln, but there were many chances to practice speaking, and sometimes there were contests with prizes. Dr. Randall hoped both the brothers would use every chance they got to learn to express themselves effectively from pulpit or platform. It was not too soon to begin.

Now it happened that Archy and Frank had a headstart in this direction, thanks to Mauma. When they were going to school to the white schoolmaster in Charleston, Mauma had bought each of them a book called a "speaker." In it were many patriotic speeches that the boys had to memorize and recite aloud for her.

They had not forgotten the words of some of the speeches. More important, they had not forgotten the feeling of confidence they had gained from so much practice. Other students had to fight against shyness when they got to their feet, but not Archy or Frank.

The first time there was an oratorical contest at Lincoln after that, Archy won first prize.

There were many people from outside the college in the audience to which Archy spoke. One was a congressman from Philadelphia named Shellenbarker. He was so impressed that he persuaded one of the city newspapers to print an article about the contest and its winner.

Archy saw his name in print for the first time, and cut the article out to send to Charleston so that Mauma and Mrs. Pillsbury could share the thrill.

But that was not the end of the matter.

About a month later, he received a letter from someone in Boston who had also seen the article. The letter was signed, A. G. Weld, and the handwriting was unfamiliar.

My maiden name was Grimké . . . as this name is a very uncommon one, it has occurred to me that you had probably been the slave of one of my brothers . . .

The letter was from Miss Angelina! A. G. Weld was Angelina Grimké, one of the abolitionist sisters Mrs. Pillsbury had talked about in Charleston and Charlotte Forten had talked about in Boston. The ones he and Frank had not wanted to visit because Miss Eliza was staying with them.

Mrs. Weld said that she felt

. . . a great desire to know all about you: who you are, whether you have any brothers and sisters, who your parents are . . . anything you want to tell me about yourself.

She told a little about herself: how she and her older sister had left Charleston because

. . . we could not endure to live in the midst of the oppression of slavery,

and how the city officials had forbidden them ever to return. She closed by asking again that Archy write and answer her.

He had a hard time deciding whether to do that or not. He still didn't want to get mixed up in any way with Eliza Grimké. Was she still at the Welds'? Or had she gone back to Charleston?

The more he thought about it, the more likely it seemed that she was gone. For she could have answered the questions Mrs. Weld was asking him.

He decided that there was really no reason not to write. But once he started, he found himself putting down things he had never meant to. He told the whole story of his father's deathbed promise, and how Montague Grimké had broken it, how cruelly he and his aunt had treated boys who they knew to be their blood kin.

All of Archy's anger and bitterness rose to the surface and poured into the letter. After he mailed it, he was almost sorry he had.

There was no reason to lash out at someone who

had done him no harm for things other white Grimkés had done. Mrs. Weld would be hurt, perhaps angry. He would not hear from her again.

But her next letter was an even bigger surprise than her first had been.

She accepted him and Frank as nephews! She invited them to come and visit her! Just as if there were no bar of color between them, no reason for those on one side of the line to hate those on the other!

There was more about her own life in this letter. She told how she and Sarah had traveled over the north, making speeches against slavery in days when mobs attacked people who did such things. She told of times when stones were thrown at them, when a hall in which she had just finished speaking was burned to the ground. Theodore Weld, the man she had married, was also a fighter against slavery, she said.

Archy understood that Mrs. Weld was telling all this so that he would trust her. She wanted him to believe that she was not like the Grimkés he had known up to now. And she was offering all sorts of help—for him and Frank, for Mauma, if she needed it, and for John.

It all sounded fine. But could he trust anyone who was friendly to Miss Eliza?

Frank felt the same way. He reminded Archy of how Eliza had talked about her two "wicked" sisters and their "crazy notions" about black people being equal to whites. Would she have gone to stay with those sisters unless she had changed her ideas? Or they had changed theirs?

It was safer to stay away from white people as much as possible, and from Grimkés above all others. Mrs. Weld might mean well, but the gulf between white and black couldn't be filled by good intentions. It was too deep.

The brothers decided to refuse the invitation and the friendship that it was supposed to seal.

The only regret Archy felt was on John's account. Mrs. Weld had sounded as if she would like to help him come north to school. It didn't look as if he was going to get that chance unless someone like her offered to pay his way. For John was not doing well enough to earn a scholarship.

But not even for such a reason did Archy want to accept favors from a white Grimké. He wrote a polite letter of refusal that should have ended the correspondence, once and for all.

That was in March.

In June there were final examinations for the year. Archy and Frank thought of nothing else until they were over, and they had received their grades.

Very good in all subjects!

While they were celebrating the victory, they were sent for by President Randall. He was waiting for them in his study, and with him was a tall, very pale, very thin, gray-haired lady. She looked so much like Archy that there was no need to guess who she was.

President Randall introduced her as Mrs. Theodore Weld, but she corrected him gently. She was their Aunt Angelina, she said, and she hoped the young men would call her that.

She took Archy's hand, then Frank's, and pressed them tightly. Then she asked Dr. Randall to leave them alone for a while.

She had come all the way to Lincoln, although she was not well and the trip had been hard for her, because she wanted to get to know her nephews and to let them know her. She seemed to guess much of what lay behind their refusal to come to her.

She could understand that they might feel ashamed of the name of Grimké after the sins committed by people who bore it. There was no way to defend what Montague had done to his half-brothers. Nor what Henry Grimké had done in leaving Mauma and her sons legally enslaved.

But she believed that Henry had acted out of love, as well as weakness. He must have loved Mauma very much, for he had left his home in Charleston

because of her. He had taken her from the city where she could be nothing but a slave, out to Cane-Acres where she was as much of a wife to him as the laws of the slave system would allow.

If he had been braver and wiser, he would have left the south, taking Mauma and his sons with him. And when he knew he was dying, he ought to have entrusted their fate to his sisters in the north who would have carried out the trust. Instead he had trusted an unworthy son.

Angelina asked Archy and Frank to pity their father for his cowardice and his bad judgment, but not to be ashamed of his name. She told them of other Grimkés, white ones, who had done things to be proud of. For instance, their uncle, Thomas, who died before they were born.

Thomas Grimké was traveling in the north when he suddenly fell ill and died. He had just talked with his abolitionist sisters, and they believed he was ready to take a stand against slavery. He had already taken a stand against breaking up the Union over it. And like his sisters, he had been threatened by mobs because of his beliefs.

He was in the South Carolina Senate at the time when he warned his fellow-citizens of what would happen if the state were to leave the Union. A mob of angry slaveowners had come to burn his house unless he took back his words. Uncle Thomas sent his family away and went out on the balcony of his house, looked down at the mob and told them to shoot, if they had the courage. But he would not take back a word.

All of his warnings had come true in the war, which had come exactly as he foresaw.

There were other Grimké uncles—Frederick, who had gone to Ohio and become a famous lawyer, and Charles, who had stayed home and lived off his family, never doing a day's useful work in his life. And there was Aunt Anna, who had freed her own slaves and gone north, but would never speak out for fear of being persecuted as Angelina and Sarah had been. And Uncle John, a doctor in Charleston, who had quarreled so bitterly with Angelina over her beliefs that he had died without ever forgiving her.

While Mrs. Weld was talking, Archy was beginning to understand something about the Grimkés—and about other white people. They were like blacks, like Westons, and O'Hears, and other families Archy knew well. There were strong hearts and weak ones in the same family circle, good people and wicked ones, and many, many who were mixtures of both.

"Our name was once honored in this land," his aunt said gravely. "Now it lies in the dust. I charge you to lift it up and set it high. Make it shine again. There is no one who can do that but you."

Archy—and Frank, too—accepted the love Aunt Angelina was offering and with it the challenge that was to shape the rest of his life.

8

A NEW FAMILY IN AMERICA

The aunts did pay for John's preparatory year at Lincoln. But John liked going to school in the north even less than he had liked it at home. He was glad at the year's end to go back to Charleston and "keep Mauma company."

After that the aunts sent small but regular gifts of money and clothes and books to Archy and Frank. When it came time for them to graduate, they were again invited to come to Boston to visit the Welds. This time they accepted.

It would be no ordinary visit. In a country that had declared that "all men are created equal" but which held some men in slavery to others, this might be the first time that a family of free white people welcomed—in public—black people, former slaves, as blood relations, kinfolk!

Archy and Frank were not ashamed of the black side of their family. They had once been ashamed of the white. Now they were learning to take pride in the good people on that side. They wanted these good people to take pride in them.

For this reason they wanted to look like members of a fine and famous family. They looked at magazines and newspapers for pictures of how young gentlemen, just out of college, dressed on formal occasions. They had no money to waste, but they scraped together enough to buy what they thought they needed.

When the great moment came and they were knocking on the door of the Welds' rather modest home, they were wearing handsome black suits, high silk hats and boots made to order, and carrying canes!

Years afterward Archy and Frank would tell the story of that day and laugh at the "airs" they were putting on. But their new aunts and uncle and cousins did not laugh.

The Welds' style of living was as simple as that of very poor people. They did not believe in spend-

ing more than was absolutely necessary on clothes or food. They enjoyed no comforts or luxuries that others could not have.

But they did not say a single word in criticism of their nephews' expensive and showy outfits. They simply opened their arms and their home in a welcome so warm that the young men didn't have time to feel embarrassed.

Next to the warmth of that welcome, the best thing about the trip to Boston, as far as Archy was concerned, was his visit to Harvard College.

He had dreamed about Harvard ever since Major Delaney had told him it was the best in the whole United States. The reality was even better than the dreams.

The campus was beautifully green with old trees and ivy. The buildings were handsome and dignified, but not so dignified that they shut strangers out. And there was a feeling of promise in the quiet air. Here, it seemed to say, you can learn anything and everything you want to learn. Here ideas and ideals can take root and grow strong so that they can stand against any winds that blow in the world outside these walls.

Before he left Boston, Archy had decided that he wanted to come to Harvard to get his law degree.

It was not going to be easy.

Even if he could pass the admissions examinations, there was the problem of money. Harvard was an expensive school. He had already taken so much help from his white aunts that he didn't want to ask any more.

Besides, he realized now that it was not entirely from choice that they lived so simply. They had spent all the money they inherited on freeing slaves, their own and their family's. Both sisters and Uncle Theodore had taught school to support themselves, but Angelina was too ill now, and Sarah was too old. What Theodore Weld earned just covered their needs. Where they had got the small amounts they had sent him and Frank, Archy didn't know. But he certainly didn't want them to sacrifice any more on his account.

Nevertheless, when his aunts found out how he felt about Harvard, they began to plan how the money could be saved. They had two years to do it in, for Archy would have to spend that much time at Lincoln before he could take the Harvard examinations. Aunt Sarah said she would start an "Archy Fund" and try her hand at writing a novel to earn money to put in it. Aunt Angelina and Uncle Theodore said they would talk to people they knew who were interested in the education of freedmen, as ex-slaves were called.

If they could get together enough to pay for Archy's first year at Harvard, they hoped he would win a scholarship that would pay for his second. It all sounded possible, if not easy.

So the brothers went back to Lincoln, back to a life of hard work and high hopes.

Frank had a new ambition, too. He had met the young lady of the Anti-Slavery Office again, and Miss Charlotte Forten now seemed just the sort of wife he wanted. But it would be at least four years before he could finish his studies and be admitted to the ministry. Not until he had a church of his own did Frank think he ought to tell "Lotty" of his hopes.

Archy was glad he only had money and study problems, and not those of a lover who hadn't declared his love and hoped his beloved would wait without knowing what she was waiting for.

The last two years at Lincoln were not as hard as the first had been. Both of the brothers had jobs that paid small salaries and that were interesting in themselves. Archy was the college librarian. Although he had little time to read for pleasure, he liked being surrounded by books. Once in a while he let himself daydream about writing a book and seeing his name in small gold letters on the narrow leather back of a volume on some library shelf.

Suddenly—or so it seemed—the two years were over. The brothers were graduating from Lincoln University with master's degrees.

Archy had been admitted to Harvard, and Frank to Princeton Theological Seminary in New Jersey. They were going to be separated again, but the end of another separation was in sight. Once he had a church, Frank was going to bring Mauma up to live with him. Archy too looked forward to having a home of his own in which Mauma could rest and enjoy the fruit of all her work and suffering and sacrificing for her sons.

During Archy's first year at Harvard Law School, Aunt Sarah died. He had the happiness of knowing that he had made her very proud of him. She wrote in a letter not long before her death that of all the sons of her many brothers and sisters, Archy and Frank were the only ones who were carrying forward the work on which she had spent her life. Also Aunt Sarah knew before she died that Archy had won the scholarship that would see him through his last year.

Now for the first time since they had been accepted into it, there was a disagreement between the brothers and their white family. Both the aunts had taken it for granted that Archy and Frank would go back to the south to practice the professions for which they were training. It was a shock to them to discover that neither of the young men had any intention of doing so.

Aunt Angelina argued that it was Archy's duty.

He and Frank had not been chosen, she said, as special pets of fortune, to make free, happier lives for themselves. They had been chosen and helped so that they could help others. They were like Moses, who had been called up to Mount Sinai to view the Promised Land, not to enter it, but to lead others to it.

Archy and Frank felt the same way about their duty to help others. But they had lived as free men in the north; they could never live as slaves again. And that was how they would have to live in the south. Slavery had never been completely abolished, and it was beginning to creep back in many different ways. There would be no freedom there to speak their minds against the enemies of freedom.

Archy tried to remind his aunt that she and her sister had to leave the south to fight for what they believed. She thought it was different now. He and Frank did not.

There seemed to be no way to resolve the disagreement by argument. Archy had to try it his way. So did Frank. Only time would tell whether they were turning their backs on the challenge they had accepted, to make the name of Grimké a proud one, or whether they were going about it in the only practical way.

9

A HARD ROW TO HOE

By the time Archy graduated from law school in 1874, he could see that there was little chance he would ever fulfill his ambition to represent his people in the United States Congress or Senate.

There had been many Negroes in high office right after the war, but there were few now, and they knew that their days in office were numbered. Instead of moving into full citizenship, Negroes were being pushed back and losing even the half-freedom they had won.

Right at the start of Archy's career, he ran into

a problem that threatened to keep him from ever practicing law. In spite of a degree with honors from the finest school in the country, he couldn't find a law firm in the city of Boston that would accept him as a clerk.

Every young lawyer began that way. When he had learned all he could from books and lectures, he went to work in some law office, doing the less interesting and important jobs, so he could learn by watching the older men. He also learned by doing, taking on more and more difficult tasks until—after a year or so—he was ready to "hang out his shingle." That was a way of saying "open an office of his own."

A lawyer who had not served a clerkship was really not ready to practice.

Archy remembered his old dream of the world of locked doors that freedom was to open. Had he unlocked this one and entered only to look around? Was he going to be pushed politely out again? And for one reason only! Because his skin was a little too dark!

At this point a new friend came to his aid. Mrs. Walling was a white woman in whose house he had rented a room while he was going to law school. When she heard about his trouble, she went to a lawyer named William Bowditch and asked him to have a talk with the young man.

Bowditch had befriended the great Negro leader, Frederick Douglass, when he first escaped from slavery. Also he had a special sympathy for a young man who bore a name already famous for things other people had done. William Bowditch was related to Nathaniel, the great Yankee sailor whose book on navigation is used by every American sea captain even today.

He consented to take young Mr. Grimké into his firm and for the next two years helped him in every way he could.

In 1876, Archibald H. Grimké and James H. Wolff announced that they were opening an office for the practice of law.

Business was poor at the start. There were not many clients brave enough to hire a Negro to represent them in court. Many Negroes didn't believe that one of their own race would be able to get justice for them from white juries or white judges. Being young was another disadvantage. Some people feel more confidence in older men just because they are older. And those who did come to the office of Grimké and Wolff as clients were often too poor to pay.

Archy found it hard to keep himself neatly dressed and still eat three times a day those first months. He couldn't help but envy Frank, who had graduated from Princeton and gone straight to a position as minister of the Fifteenth Church in Washington, D.C. Frank had married his Lotty less than six months later.

By this time Archy was also in love and planning to be married.

Sarah Stanley was the daughter of a white minister who had supported Lincoln's policy of emancipation and thought of himself as a believer in equality for all men. But he was not ready to give his consent to the marriage of his daughter to a Negro, not even one as intelligent and well-educated and handsome as Archibald Grimké.

None of the bride's family came to the wedding, which took place in Boston in 1879.

In spite of this, and other ways in which the marriage got off to a bad start, Archy was determined to make a good life for his wife and the baby girl born to them in 1880. She was christened Angelina Weld Grimké, after Aunt Angelina who had died only a few months before her birth.

On the baby's account the young Grimkés moved to a suburb, near the Weld home. They had the second floor of a house owned by white people who soon became warm and loyal friends. Things were not easy, but on the whole they seemed to be getting better.

That is, for Archy personally.

For the Negro people, north and south, things were getting worse. Archy sat up late at night writing articles about what was happening. Many of them were published in Boston newspapers, like the *Herald* and the *Traveler*. They drew attention to the writer, but Archy couldn't see that they had any other result.

He and his new law partner, Butler Wilson, began to think about starting a newspaper of their own that would give a voice to the Negro as Major Delaney's paper and Frederick Douglass' *North Star* had done before the war. They knew such a paper would never pay them for the work they would have to put into it, but their law practice was doing better. Neither of the partners was getting rich, but at least they were not going hungry.

So, in 1883, these new editors brought out the first issue of a new paper that they called *The Hub*.

At least one of Archy's ambitions was fulfilled, and he was very proud of the paper and of his name on its "masthead." He wished his aunts could have seen it. Uncle Theodore assured him that they would have been proud, too.

The Hub attracted favorable attention all over New England. People began to think of Archibald Grimké as the spokesman of the Negro. He was consulted by politicians, invited to sit on committees, and approached by important members of the Republican Party who wanted him to help them win Negro votes. His private law business picked up, too, so that there was more work than he could handle without working many nights.

Suddenly, in the midst of all this interesting and useful activity, Archy's life was shattered by an explosion in its very center. His young wife left him, taking the baby Angelina with her.

The forces that had been working silently and steadily against his marriage had grown too strong. Sarah Stanley Grimké could not stand the terrible pressure of prejudice. It bore down on her until she felt like a criminal. Indeed, in some states of the Union she and Archy would have broken the law by marrying.

In the year of their wedding, Virginia had passed a law declaring that a marriage between a white person and a black one was not legal.

For more than a year, the confused and tortured young woman tried to make a life for herself and her child in the home of her father, in Michigan. Reverend Stanley tried to help. He had overcome his first feeling of opposition. He respected his son-in-law and adored his little granddaughter. But Sarah needed more support than he could give her.

At last she sent little Angelina back to Archibald and began a tragic life of wandering over the world, seeking and never finding happiness, regretting more and more bitterly the lack of courage that had destroyed her marriage and her motherhood.

Archibald kept himself from despair by concentrating on being both mother and father to his little girl. He could not make a real home for her without a wife, but he could love her as Mauma had loved him and his brothers, when she had to be two parents in one.

He kept himself too busy with work on behalf of others to think much about himself. And there was plenty of work for a lawyer and a writer dedicated to the welfare of Negro Americans in the terrible 1880's and 1890's.

In the south, Negro farmers were being turned off land they had been working ever since the war, believing it was their own. The old white owners were reclaiming it. It had been taken from them to punish them for having rebelled against the Union. But now the government had declared "amnesty," which meant forgiveness to all former rebels. Forgiveness and their property back!

Black men had a choice between going somewhere else—and where was there to go if one had no money to buy land?—or working for their old

masters at wages just high enough to keep them from starving.

In the cities of the south, Negroes were losing the right to vote. Sometimes the excuse was that they had made a bad use of their new rights, that they needed more education before they could be good citizens and vote wisely. But less and worse—not more and better—education was being offered to them.

Negro children were no longer admitted to the same schools as white ones. In some places there were no schools for them at all. In others their schools were no better than those Archy had gone to in secret in slavery days.

Worst of all, white and black were being separated so completely that the chance of their ever knowing and accepting each other was being killed.

A new phrase was heard in America. Jim Crow! It had once been a dance. Now it was a system of laws and customs for keeping Negroes away from white people. Out of all but the worst-paying jobs! Out of hotels and barber shops and restaurants where white people went. Out of public libraries and hospitals! Out of all but the back seats in streetcars and trains!

And no one was making his voice heard in protest against all this.

In the south Negroes who resisted—or white people who objected—paid a terrible price. Night-riders
burned their houses, whipped, and sometimes mur-
dered them.

In the north, the old abolitionists were nearly all
dead. People who thought they believed in equality
were tired of hearing about "the Negro problem."
Newspapers like *The Hub* were needed more than
ever, but there was no money to be found to support
them.

It was what Mauma used to call "a hard row to
hoe," and it seemed to stretch ahead into the future
as far as Archy could see.

10

HONOR AND HONORS

In 1899 Archibald Grimké was fifty years old.

He had spent twenty-five years getting an education to prepare himself for the work he wanted to do and twenty-five years at work. It was time to take stock of what he had done with half of his life.

First of all, he had raised a daughter of whom he was very proud. Young Angelina was going to be a teacher when she finished college, and she was showing promise of being a fine poet as well. Her father had done a good job on her up-bringing, but he couldn't take all the credit for the results.

For she had a second pair of parents in her Uncle Frank and Aunt Lotty. They had lost their only child while she was still a baby and had always looked on their niece as a foster child. Since the parsonage of the Fifteenth Street Church in Washington was large, they had been able to give a home to Mauma, who had come up from Charleston to spend her last years in honor and comfort, and also to Angelina whenever she needed one.

Because he could leave his child so well loved and looked after, Archibald had been able to accept what was so far the greatest honor of his life. He had been appointed by President Cleveland to be United States Consul to the island republic of Santo Domingo. Although he was not the first man of his race to be sent abroad as the official representative of his country, there had not been many before him and none had done a better job.

His old dream about seeing his name on the cover of a book had come true. A publishing firm had asked him to write the lives of two great white abolitionists: William Lloyd Garrison and Senator Charles Sumner. He had wondered then whether Aunt Angelina would have been satisfied that he had made the name of Grimké shine again.

Perhaps. But he was not satisfied.

He had done better for himself than he had for his people. He had won honors, though not much wealth. But he had done nothing that made any impression on the tide that was running harder than ever against men of dark skin in the land of the free.

There were times when white men seemed to go crazy with fear and hatred of black men. Twenty-five hundred Negroes had been lynched in the last fifteen years, killed by mobs who took the law into their own hands.

Sometimes these mobs broke into a jail where a Negro accused of a crime was waiting for a trial. They would try him by "lynch law," condemn him without any proof but their own suspicions, and punish him by death. Sometimes their victim was not accused of any crime but being too independent, not polite enough to white men. And sometimes when mobs got excited, they caught and killed the wrong man, one they were not even looking for.

Lynchings began in the south, but they were happening in the north, too. And no one had yet been punished for taking part in one.

As the new century began, something even more frightening than lynchings began to occur in America, north as well as south. First in one small town, then another, then in a great city, then in an army camp—white people got worked up into a frenzy of rage not against one particular Negro, but against Negroes in general.

Race riots were disgracing America in the eyes of the world. Horrible acts of cruelty were committed in them, against old and young, women and children, humble and proud. Anyone with a dark skin was the enemy!

Homes in Negro neighborhoods were wrecked and burned. Families were driven from places they had lived all their lives. Businesses and shops were destroyed while policemen and sheriffs stood by and watched. Some of them were on the side of the mobs. Others knew that if they interfered, the mob might turn on them. White men had been lynched for being "nigger lovers."

Something had to be done!

Archibald Grimké threw himself into the fight with the only weapons he had—his voice and his pen.

He wrote article after article, denouncing the violence and injustice, and pleading that the Negro be allowed to vote. Only by having the vote and using it could he defend himself! Only by making democracy real for all her citizens could America defend her great dream!

His articles were printed in the most important magazines of the country. Some were made into little books, and published by the American Negro Academy, of which he was made president. But year by year the war against the Negro went on, a war in which all the weapons that counted were on one side.

Clearly it was too big a job for any one man, or even for many men acting independently. Negroes and whites who believed in equal rights had to band together. They had to organize.

A few brave Negro leaders had tried to form such organizations before the turn of the century, but none of them had lasted. They had found no way to reach the ears of the thousands of black men who ought to have joined. And white men of good will seemed to have gone deaf.

What would it take to make them hear?

In 1905 a call was sent out by a young Negro professor named William E. B. DuBois. He asked twenty-nine other prominent and well-educated members of the race to meet with him on the Canadian side of Niagara Falls. Archibald Grimké was one of those invited, and he went.

The founders of the Niagara Movement drew up a declaration of their demands: freedom of speech; the vote for all adult men, regardless of color; an end to all discrimination based on race; recognition of the principles of human brotherhood; and respect for the working man.

They met the next year and the next. Each time there were more of them, and they issued a louder, clearer, braver appeal. But they were generals without an army. Declarations and appeals were not enough.

Then in 1909 the worst race riot in America's history took place in Springfield, Illinois, the town where Lincoln had lived and where he is buried. Now at last white people were shocked into action.

A man named William English Walling wrote an article called "Race War in the North." A grandson of William Lloyd Garrison and a white woman social worker named Mary Ovington read it and wrote Walling saying they wanted to join him in doing something to end this war.

A conference was called. Many famous white people came. So did most of the members of the Niagara Movement. Out of this meeting a new organization was born. It was called the National Association for the Advancement of Colored People.

Here, in his sixtieth year, Archibald Grimké found use for all the knowledge and skill and experience he had gained on behalf of the people he wanted to serve.

He became chairman of the Washington, D.C., branch of the N.A.A.C.P. as well as a national vice-president of the organization. His legal talents were

used in battles waged in federal courts of the capital. His talent as a writer was used in articles and pamphlets calling the attention of white and black citizens to what he called

THE SHAME OF AMERICA

. . . Be not deceived, friends. Let us like brave men and women face the stern reality of our situation . . .

. . . The North and South are in substantial accord in respect to us and the position we are to occupy in this land.

. . . We are to be forever treated as an alien race, allowed to live here in strict subordination to the white race.

. . . We are to hew for it wood, draw for it water, till for it the earth . . . black for it boots, run for it errands, receive from it kicks and crumbs . . .

. . . No one can save us from such a fate but God . . . but ourselves!

Before Archibald Grimké retired from active work he had seen the N.A.A.C.P. win three important victories in the United States Supreme Court: state laws that kept Negroes from voting had been declared unconstitutional; city laws that forced Negroes to live in certain sections only had been declared null and void; and decisions of all-white juries against Negro defendants had been set aside as unfair.

Mr. Grimké had his share in these victories as well as in others that were still hidden in the future. For he had done much to build the organization that was going to carry on the same struggle for as long as it was necessary.

In recognition of this, the N.A.A.C.P. celebrated his seventieth year by honoring him with the Arthur B. Spingarn Medal, given each year to the man who has made the greatest contribution to the cause of equality for minority people in the United States.

There was no longer any doubt that he had made the name Grimké shine by the work his aunts believed he was called for, just as they had been called in their time.

Work toward "liberty and justice for all!"

INDEX